Summer Vacation
Internet Research Projects (Grades 5-8)

Who is Susan B. Anthony?

Use a laptop, tablet or phone to access the internet and explore **Susan B. Anthony**. Record five interesting facts you learned about this famous American and why we celebrate her birthday on February 15th.

1
2
3
4
5

Countries in Europe

Use a phone, tablet or laptop to identify some of the largest and most populous countries in Europe:

Austria, Azerbaijan, Belarus, Belgium, Bulgaria, Croatia, Czech Republic, Denmark, England, Finland, France, Russia, Greece, Hungary, Ireland, Kazakhstan, Italy, Netherlands, Norway, Poland, Portugal, Romania, Scotland, Serbia, Slovakia, Spain, Sweden, Switzerland, Turkey, Ukraine, Wales

What do we know about space travel?

Use a computer, tablet or phone to search online for answers to this question.

1
2
3
4
5
6
7

ONLINE SOURCES OF INFORMATION

1)
2)
3)

101 printable activities

C. Mahoney

Life is about choices...

What do we know about space travel?

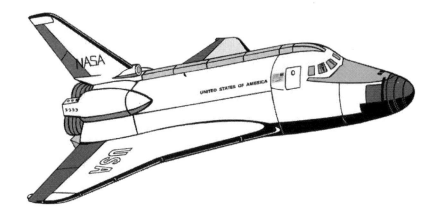

Use a <u>computer</u>, <u>tablet</u> or <u>phone</u> to search online for answers to this question.

1

2

3

4

5

6

7

ONLINE SOURCES OF INFORMATION:

1)	2)	3)

Who is Susan B. Anthony?

Use a <u>laptop</u>, <u>tablet</u> or <u>phone</u> to access the internet and explore **Susan B. Anthony**. Record five interesting facts you learned about this famous American and why we celebrate her birthday on February 15th.

1

2

3

4

5

Giant's Causeway

Search for interesting facts about this Irish tourist destination. What are its most interesting features? Why do people travel there and explore? What is so amazing about this place?

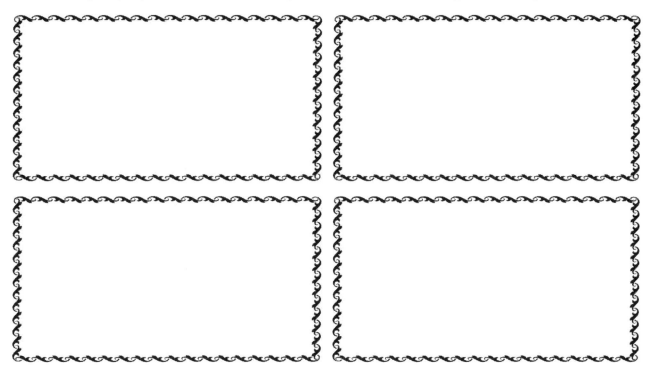

ONLINE SOURCES OF INFORMATION:

_____

_____

What do we know about Black Holes?

Use a <u>computer</u>, <u>tablet</u> or <u>phone</u> to search online for answers to this question.

1

2

3

4

5

ONLINE SOURCES OF INFORMATION:

Japan's Flag

Draw the national flag of Japan. Use colored pencils, crayons, or markers. Be neat and accurate.

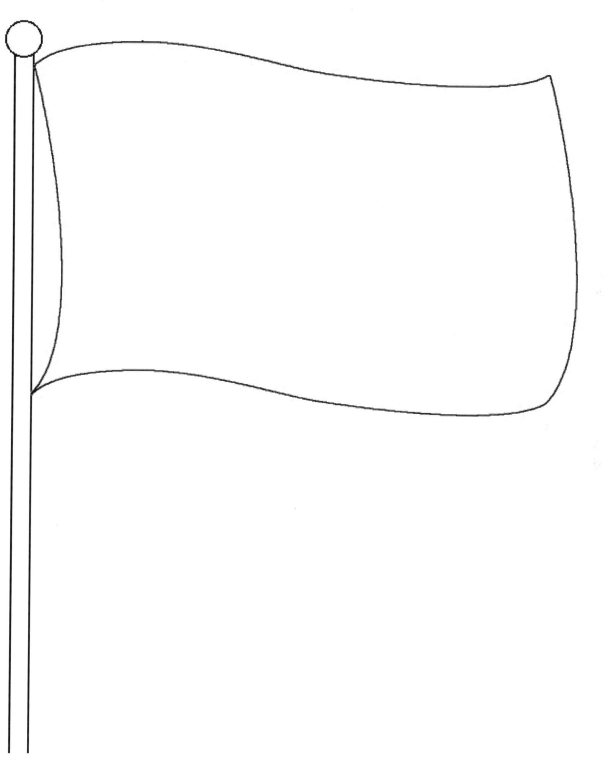

Countries in Europe

Use a phone, tablet or laptop to identify some of the largest and most populous countries in Europe:

Austria, Azerbaijan, Belarus, Belgium, Bulgaria, Croatia, Czech Republic, Denmark, England, Finland, France, Russia, Greece, Hungary, Ireland, Kazakhstan, Italy, Netherlands, Norway, Poland, Portugal, Romania, Scotland, Serbia, Slovakia, Spain, Sweden, Switzerland, Turkey, Ukraine, Wales

The Saber-toothed Cat
California State Fossil

Use a <u>laptop</u>, <u>tablet</u> or <u>phone</u> to access the internet and explore this **fossil**. Record several interesting facts you discovered in your research.

1

2

3

4

5

6

7

SOURCES:

_____

_____

A Stamp from China

Search online for an interesting stamp from China. Use colored pencils, crayons or markers as you draw this stamp. Be neat and accurate.

The Rat

Use a phone, tablet or laptop to answer these questions.

Is the rat dangerous to humans?

☐ – YES

☐ – NO

What does a rat eat?

Is a rat smart?

Yes OR **No**

How long does a rat live?

ONLINE SOURCES OF INFORMATION:

1)	2)	3)

Coat of Arms of China

Draw the Coat of Arms of China. Use colored pencils, crayons, or markers. Be neat and accurate.

Who is Frederick Douglass?

Use a phone, tablet or laptop to find five important facts.

1. _____
_____
_____
SOURCE: _____

2. _____
_____
_____
SOURCE: _____

3. _____
_____
_____
SOURCE: _____

4. _____
_____
_____
SOURCE: _____

5. _____
_____
_____
SOURCE: _____

Countries in Latin America

Use a phone, tablet or laptop to identify 22 Latin American countries:

Argentina, Belize, Bolivia, Brazil, Chile, Colombia, Costa Rica, Dominican Republic, Ecuador, El Salvador, French Guiana, Guatemala, Guyana, Honduras, Mexico, Nicaragua, Panama, Paraguay, Peru, Suriname, Uruguay, and Venezuela

Money from Russia

Search online for an interesting coin from Russia. Use colored pencils, crayons or markers as you draw this coin. Be neat and accurate.

Illinois

Use a phone, tablet or laptop to answer these questions.

1. What is the state motto? _____
2. How many people live there? _____
3. How big is this state? _____
4. Who is the governor? _____
5. Where is the capitol? _____
6. Which city is the largest? _____
7. How long have they been a state? _____
8. What job or work is most common? _____
9. What religion is most popular? _____

10. What are three interesting things you learned? _____
_____
_____
_____
_____
_____
_____
_____
_____
_____

SOURCE: _____
SOURCE: _____
SOURCE: _____

What is Lou Gehrig's Disease?

Use a <u>computer</u>, <u>tablet</u> or <u>phone</u> to search online for answers to this question.

1

2

3

4

5

ONLINE SOURCES OF INFORMATION:

1)	2)	3)

Who is Gwyneth Paltrow?

Use a laptop, tablet or phone to access the internet and explore this famous Californian.

Age:

Gender:

Place of birth:

Ethnicity:

Search for interesting facts about this famous Californian: major accomplishments in life, odd jobs, family and marriage, childhood experiences, accidents, anything that you find odd or strange:

1

2

3

4

ONLINE SOURCES OF INFORMATION:

_____

_____

The Culture of Japan

Use a phone, tablet or laptop to discover interesting facts about this country.

Food

Music

Clothing

Sports

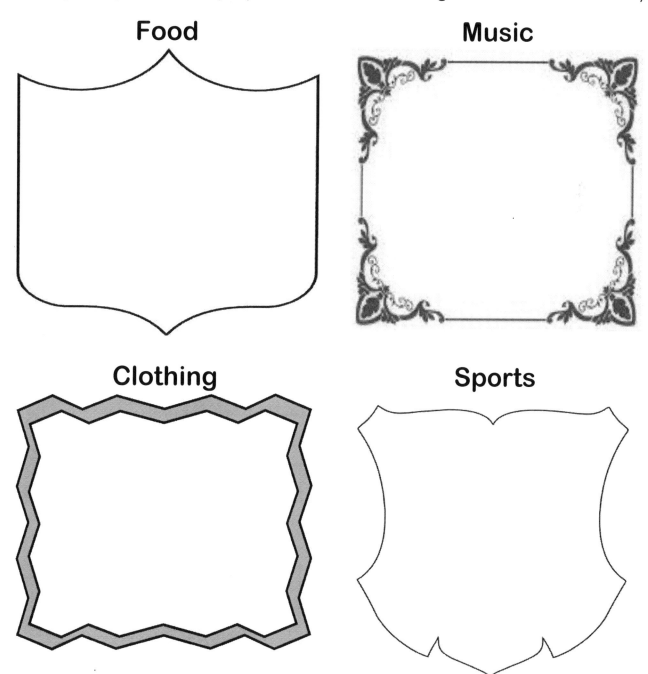

A Stamp from Israel

Search online for an interesting stamp from Israel. Use colored pencils, crayons or markers as you draw this stamp. Be neat and accurate.

Countries in Africa

Use a phone, tablet or laptop to identify some of the largest and most populous countries in Africa:

Algeria, Angola, Camaroon, Chad, Congo, Egypt, Ethiopia, Ghana, Ivory Coast, Kenya, Liberia, Libya, Madagascar, Mali, Morocco, Mozambique, Niger, Nigeria, Rwanda, Senegal, Sierra Leone, Somalia, South Africa, Sudan, Tanzania, Uganda, Zaire, Zambia, and Zimbabwe

The Indigenous Peoples of America

1.

2.

3.

4.

5.

6.

7.

8.

9.

10.

ONLINE SOURCES OF INFORMATION:

1)	2)	3)

The Hermit Crab

Use a phone, tablet or laptop to answer these questions.

Is the hermit crab dangerous to humans?

☐ – YES

☐ – NO

_____
_____
_____
_____

How does a hermit crab eat?

_____
_____
_____
_____

Is a hermit crab smart?

YES
NO

_____
_____
_____

How long does a hermit crab live?

_____
_____
_____

24
365
7

ONLINE SOURCES OF INFORMATION:

⬇

1) _____

2) _____

3) _____

The Map of Illinois

Use a phone, tablet or laptop to identify important places in this state: mountains, rivers, lakes, cities, historical sites, neighboring states, or bordering bodies of water.

Who is Dennis Hopper?

Use a laptop, tablet or phone to access the internet and explore this famous Californian.

Age:

Gender:

Place of birth:

Ethnicity:

Search for interesting facts about this famous Californian: major accomplishments in life, odd jobs, family and marriage, childhood experiences, accidents, anything that you find odd or strange:

ONLINE SOURCES OF INFORMATION:

What is the job of the President?

List ten activities or actions that a President is responsible for:

1.

2.

3.

4.

5.

6.

7.

8.

9.

10.

SOURCES:

_____

_____

Poisonous Bugs

Use a phone, tablet or laptop to answer these questions.

1. Why does a spider bite? _____

_____

_____

source #1: _____

source #2: _____

2. What happens to a honeybee that stings you? _____

_____

_____

source #1: _____

source #2: _____

3. How does a centipede defend itself? _____

_____

_____

source #1: _____

source #2: _____

4. How does a scorpion capture prey? _____

_____

_____

source #1: _____

source #2: _____

5. Why does a fire ant sting hurt? _____

_____

_____

source #1: _____

source #2: _____

Who is Andrew Jackson?

Use a phone, tablet or laptop to learn five facts about this president and why he is remembered today.

1 _____

2 _____

3 _____

4 _____

5 _____

SOURCES:

_____

A Stamp from Japan

Search online for an interesting stamp from Japan. Use colored pencils, crayons or markers as you draw this stamp. Be neat and accurate.

Distance

Use a phone, tablet or laptop to answer these questions.

1. How far must a runner run in a **marathon**? _____

_____

source #1: _____
source #2: _____

2. How far away is the **moon**? _____

_____

source #1: _____
source #2: _____

3. How far away is the **sun**? _____

_____

source #1: _____
source #2: _____

4. How far away is the nearest **star** in the sky? _____

_____

source #1: _____
source #2: _____

5. How **big** is the Milky Way Galaxy? _____

_____

source #1: _____
source #2: _____

6. What is the distance around the **earth**? _____

_____

source #1: _____
source #2: _____

California Landscape

Search online for information about the landscape of California and how it made traveling <u>easy</u> or <u>difficult</u> for the "forty-niners". Write about the mountains, the rivers, the deserts, the coasts, and what people had to do in order to get from there to here.

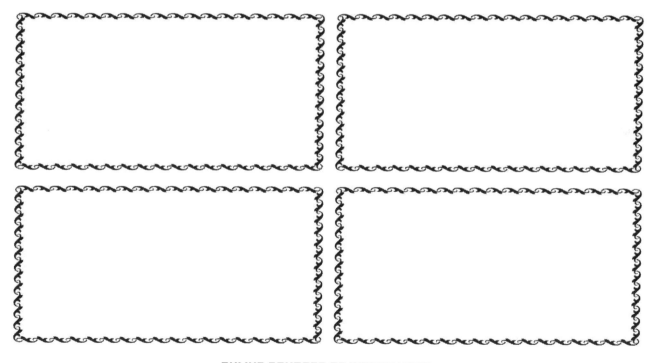

ONLINE SOURCES OF INFORMATION:

_____

_____

The Coat of Arms of Russia

Draw the Coat of Arms of Russia. Use colored pencils, crayons, or markers. Be neat and accurate.

Who is Robert Hooke?

Use a phone, tablet or laptop to answer these questions.

1. When and where was he born? _____

_____

SOURCE: _____

2. What type of work did he do? _____

_____

SOURCE: _____

3. What did he contribute to science? _____

_____

_____

_____

_____

_____

_____

_____

_____

_____

_____

SOURCE: _____

Illinois' Flag

Draw the **state flag** of Illinois. Use colored pencils, crayons, or markers. Be neat and accurate.

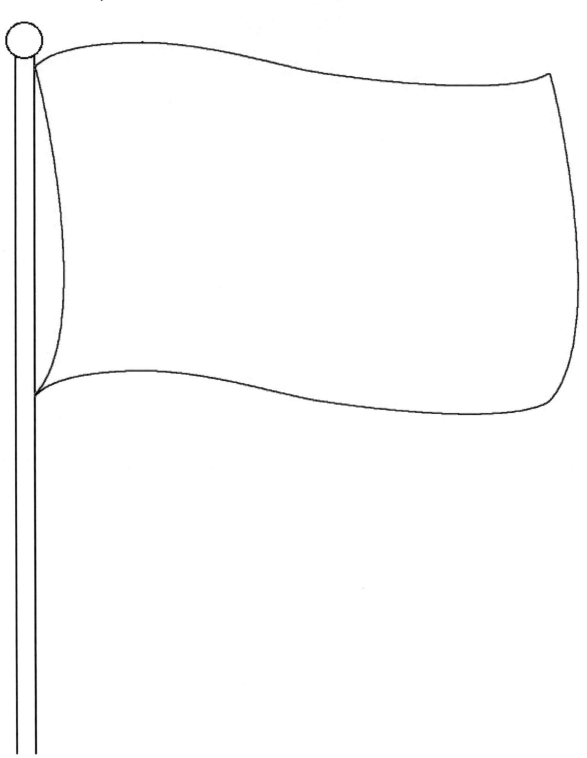

Who is Leonardo da Vinci?

Use a phone, tablet or laptop to find five important facts.

1. _____
_____
_____
SOURCE: _____

2. _____
_____
_____
SOURCE: _____

3. _____
_____
_____
SOURCE: _____

4. _____
_____
_____
SOURCE: _____

5. _____
_____
_____
SOURCE: _____

Mexico

Use a phone, tablet or laptop to learn interesting facts about this country.

Sources:

Hawaii's Islands

Use a phone, tablet or laptop to identify important places in this state: mountains, rivers, lakes, cities, historical sites, neighboring states, or bordering bodies of water.

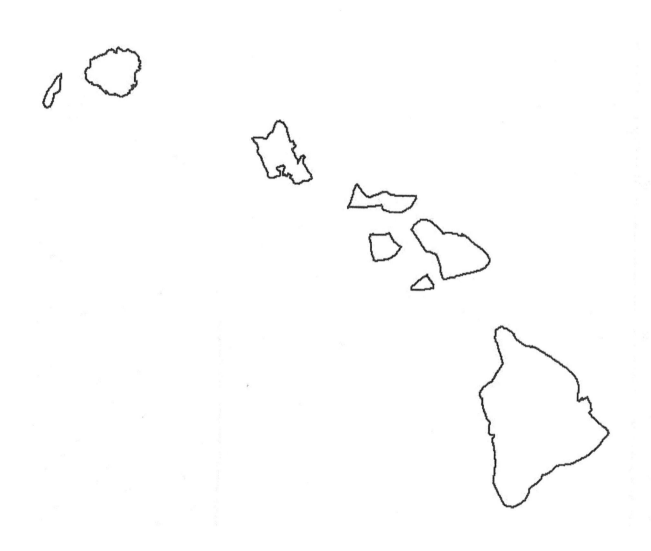

The Earth

Use a phone, tablet or laptop to answer these questions.

1. How big is the Earth? _____
_____
_____
SOURCE: _____

2. How big is the Moon? _____
_____
_____
SOURCE: _____

3. How big is the Sun? _____
_____
_____
SOURCE: _____

4. How many miles is it from the Atlantic to the Pacific Ocean?
_____
_____
SOURCE: _____

5. How many miles is it from Canada to Mexico? _____
_____
_____
SOURCE: _____

Historical Facts about Russia

Use a phone, tablet or laptop to discover interesting facts about the history of Russia: wars, disasters, laws, accomplishments, challenges…

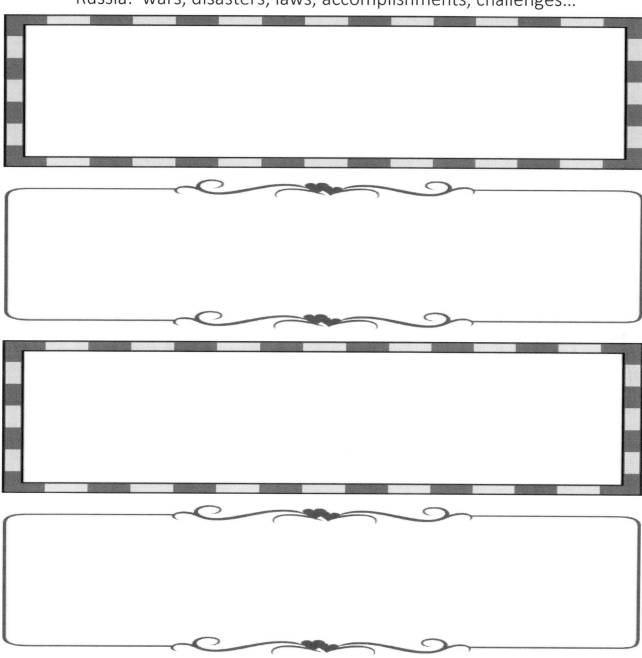

Who is Mary Leakey?

Use a phone, tablet or laptop to learn five facts about this scientist and why she is remembered today.

1 _____

2 _____

3 _____

4 _____

5 _____

SOURCES:

_____

_____

Money from Japan

Search online for an interesting coin from Japan. Use colored pencils, crayons or markers as you draw this coin. Be neat and accurate.

Facts about Egypt

Search online for interesting facts about Egypt's land and people.

_____

_____

_____

_____

_____

_____

_____

_____

_____

_____

_____

_____

_____

_____

_____

_____

_____

_____

ONLINE SOURCES OF INFORMATION:

1)	2)	3)

Germany

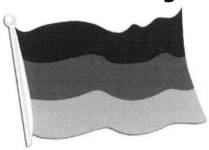

Use a phone, tablet or laptop to answer these questions.

1. What language do they speak? _____

2. How many people live there? _____

3. How big is this country? _____

4. Who is their leader? _____

5. Where is the capitol? _____

6. What kind of money do they use? _____

7. How long have they been a nation? _____

8. What religions are most common? _____

9. What sport is most popular? _____

10. What are three interesting things you learned? _____
_____
_____
_____
_____
_____
_____
_____
_____

SOURCE: _____

SOURCE: _____

SOURCE: _____

Countries in Asia

Use a phone, tablet or laptop to identify some of the largest and most populous countries in Asia:

Afghanistan, Bangladesh, China, Cambodia, Hong Kong, India, Indonesia, Iran, Iraq, Isreal, Japan, Jordan, Kazakhstan, Laos, Lebanon, Malyasia, Mongolia, Myanmar, Nepal, North Korea, Oman, Pakistan, Philippines, Qatar, Russia, Saudi Arabia, Singapore, South Korea, Syria, Taiwan, Thailand, Turkey, United Arab Empirates, Uzbekistan, Vietnam, Yemen

Who is Dwight D. Eisenhower?

Use a phone, tablet or laptop to learn five facts about this president
and why he is remembered today.

1

2

3

4

5

SOURCES:

The State Seal of Illinois

Draw the **Seal** or **Coat of Arms** for this state. Use colored pencils, crayons, or markers. Be neat and accurate.

The Bullfrog

Use a phone, tablet or laptop to answer these questions.

What it eats…

Fact #1: _____

_____

Fact #2: _____

_____

SOURCE: _____

Where it lives…

Fact #1: _____

_____

Fact #2: _____

_____

SOURCE: _____

Family life…

Fact #1: _____

_____

Fact #2: _____

_____

SOURCE: _____

Connection to humans…

Fact #1: _____

_____

Fact #2: _____

_____

SOURCE: _____

Historical Facts about Japan

Use a phone, tablet or laptop to discover interesting facts about the history of Japan: wars, disasters, laws, accomplishments, challenges...

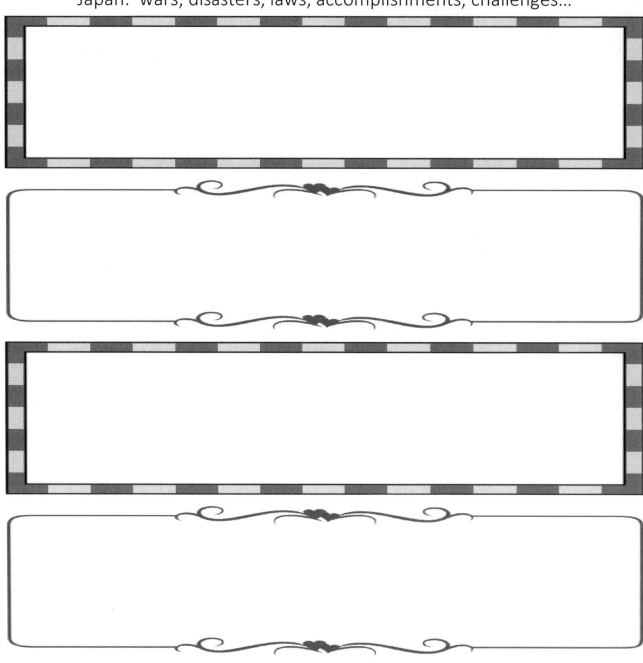

The Ostrich

Use a phone, tablet or laptop to answer these questions.

What it eats…

Fact #1: _____

_____

Fact #2: _____

_____

SOURCE: _____

Where it lives…

Fact #1: _____

_____

Fact #2: _____

_____

SOURCE: _____

Family life…

Fact #1: _____

_____

Fact #2: _____

_____

SOURCE: _____

Connection to humans…

Fact #1: _____

_____

Fact #2: _____

_____

SOURCE: _____

Historical Facts about Israel

Use a phone, tablet or laptop to discover interesting facts about the history of Israel: wars, disasters, laws, accomplishments, challenges...

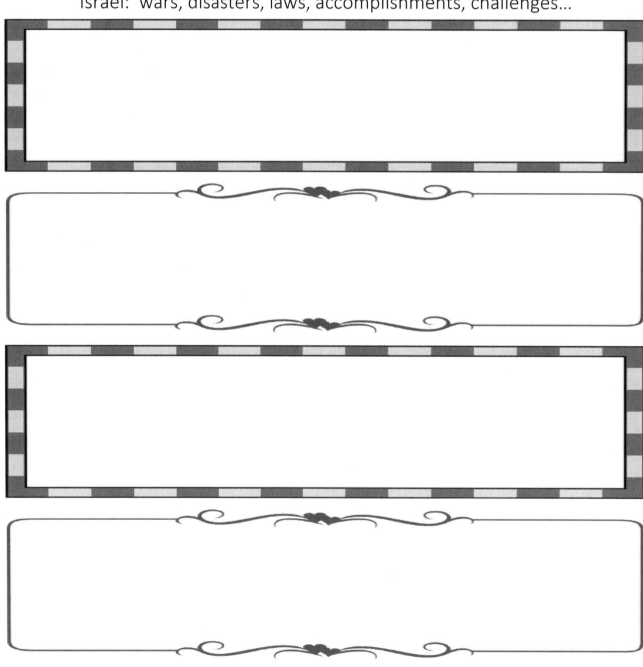

Illinois

Search online for odd or weird facts about Illinois.

_____

_____

_____

_____

_____

_____

_____

_____

_____

_____

_____

_____

_____

SOURCE: _____

SOURCE: _____

SOURCE: _____

Animals of the Tropical Rain Forest

The Caribbean Islands

Use a phone, tablet or laptop to identify some of the largest and most populous countries in the Caribbean:

Aruba, the Bahamas, Barbados, Cuba, Curacao, Cayman Islands, Dominican Republic, Grenada, Haiti, Jamaica, Martinique, Puerto Rico, Saint Lucia, Trinidad and Tobago, U.S. Virgin Islands

The State Seal of Alaska

Draw the **Seal** or **Coat of Arms** for this state. Use colored pencils, crayons, or markers. Be neat and accurate.

Geography of Israel

Use a phone, tablet or laptop to identify important places in this country: mountains, rivers, lakes, oceans or seas, cities, historical sites, neighboring countries.

Who is Harriet Tubman?

Use a phone, tablet or laptop to list five important facts.

1. _____
_____
_____
SOURCE: _____

2. _____
_____
_____
SOURCE: _____

3. _____
_____
_____
SOURCE: _____

4. _____
_____
_____
SOURCE: _____

5. _____
_____
_____
SOURCE: _____

Square Dancing

California State Folk Dance

Use a <u>laptop</u>, <u>tablet</u> or <u>phone</u> to access the internet and explore this **dance**. Record several interesting facts you discovered in your research.

SOURCES:

_____

_____

New York

Use a phone, tablet or laptop to answer these questions.

1. What is the state motto? _____
2. How many people live there? _____
3. How big is this state? _____
4. Who is the governor? _____
5. Where is the capitol? _____
6. Which city is the largest? _____
7. How long have they been a state? _____
8. What job or work is most common? _____
9. What religion is most popular? _____

10. What are three interesting things you learned? _____

_____
_____
_____
_____
_____
_____
_____
_____

SOURCE: _____
SOURCE: _____
SOURCE: _____

Coat of Arms of Japan

Draw the Coat of Arms of Japan. Use colored pencils, crayons, or markers. Be neat and accurate.

The Hummingbird

Use a phone, tablet or laptop to answer these questions.

Is the hummingbird dangerous to humans?

☐ – YES

☐ – NO

_____
_____
_____

How does a hummingbird eat?

_____
_____
_____

Is a hummingbird smart?

YES
NO

_____
_____
_____

How long does a hummingbird live?

_____
_____
_____

source: _____

source: _____

source: _____

Mexico's Flag

Draw the Flag of Mexico

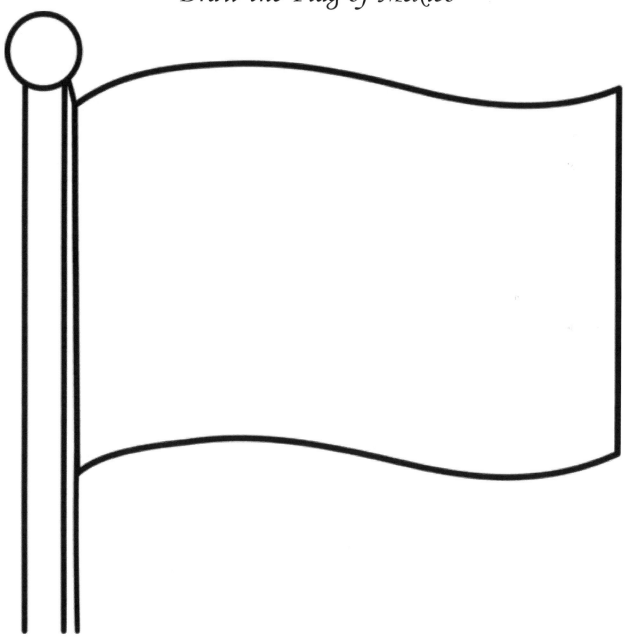

Famous People from Japan

Ireland's Geography

Use a phone, tablet or laptop to identify important places in this country.

Mountains: _____

Rivers: _____

Lakes: _____

Oceans: _____

Cities: _____

_____

Historical sites: _____

_____

Who is Ronald Reagan?

Use a phone, tablet or laptop to answer these questions.

1. When and where was he born? _____

_____

_____

SOURCE: _____

2 What type of work did he do before the presidency? _____

_____

_____

SOURCE: _____

3. Describe several of his accomplishments: _____

_____

_____

_____

_____

_____

_____

_____

_____

_____

_____

_____

SOURCE: _____

U.S. Stamp honoring Illinois

Search online for an interesting **stamp** honoring Illinois. Use colored pencils, crayons or markers as you draw this stamp. Be neat and accurate.

Deer

Use a phone, tablet or laptop to answer these questions.

What it eats…

Fact #1: _____

_____

Fact #2: _____

_____

SOURCE: _____

Where it lives…

Fact #1: _____

_____

Fact #2: _____

_____

SOURCE: _____

Family life…

Fact #1: _____

_____

Fact #2: _____

_____

SOURCE: _____

Connection to humans…

Fact #1: _____

_____

Fact #2: _____

_____

SOURCE: _____

Facts about Puerto Rico

Use a phone, tablet or laptop to discover eight interesting facts.

1

2

3

4

5

6

7

8

Sources:

A Stamp from Russia

Search online for an interesting stamp from Russia. Use colored pencils, crayons or markers as you draw this stamp. Be neat and accurate.

The Mountain Lion

Use a phone, tablet or laptop to answer these questions.

Is the mountain lion dangerous to humans?

☐ – YES

☐ – NO

How does a mountain lion eat?

Is a mountain lion smart?

YES
NO

How long does a mountain lion live?

24
365
7

ONLINE SOURCES OF INFORMATION:

1)

2)

3)

James Madison

Use a phone, tablet or laptop to find five important facts.

1. _____
_____
_____
SOURCE: _____

2. _____
_____
_____
SOURCE: _____

3. _____
_____
_____
SOURCE: _____

4. _____
_____
_____
SOURCE: _____

5. _____
_____
_____
SOURCE: _____

The State Seal of Hawaii

Draw the **Seal** or **Coat of Arms** for this state. Use colored pencils, crayons, or markers. Be neat and accurate.

Who is Ida B. Wells?

Use a phone, tablet or laptop to discover why we honor this person.

_____

_____

_____

_____

_____

_____

_____

_____

_____

_____

_____

_____

_____

_____

_____

_____

ONLINE SOURCES OF INFORMATION:

⬇

1)	2)	3)

Historical Facts about Illinois

Use a phone, tablet or laptop to discover interesting facts about the history of Illinois: wars, disasters, laws, accomplishments, challenges...

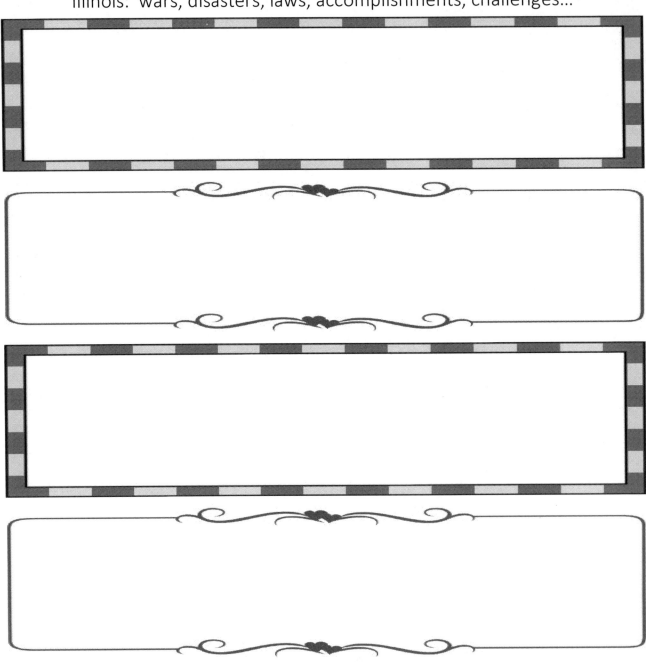

Hawaii

Use a phone, tablet or laptop to learn interesting facts about this state.

Draw the flag for this state.

List five facts you discovered:

1.

2.

3.

4.

5.

List five common wild animals.

List three crops that grow in this state.

Draw a picture that best describes this state.

Sources: _____

_____

The Sea Snake

Use a phone, tablet or laptop to answer these questions.

Is the sea snake dangerous to humans?

☐ – YES _____
☐ – NO _____
        _____
        _____

How does a sea snake eat?

_____
_____
_____

Is a sea snake smart?

YES
OR
NO _____
        _____
        _____

How long does a sea snake live?

_____
_____
_____
_____

source: _____

source: _____

source: _____

Madagascar

Use a phone, tablet or laptop to discover interesting facts about Madagascar.

_____
_____
_____
_____
_____
_____
_____
_____
_____
_____
_____
_____
_____
_____
_____
_____
_____
_____
_____
_____
_____

Sea Life

Use a phone, tablet or laptop to answer these questions.

How long does this animal live?

shark: _____

jelly fish: _____

sea cucumber: _____

walrus: _____

Where is this animal is born?

sea turtle: _____

sea lion: _____

great white shark: _____

clown fish: _____

What does this animal eat?

crab: _____

seagull: _____

gray whale: _____

stingray: _____

What covers the outside of this animal?

lobster: _____

octopus: _____

seal: _____

sea star: _____

U.S. Coin honoring Illinois

Search online for the **U.S. quarter** that honors Illinois. Use colored pencils, crayons or markers as you draw the back of this coin. Be neat and accurate.

Things I learned about Canada

Use a phone, tablet or laptop to learn interesting facts about Canada.

_____

_____

_____

_____

_____

_____

_____

_____

_____

_____

_____

_____

_____

_____

_____

_____

_____

_____

_____

_____

_____

_____

Sources: _____

Old Spanish National Historic Trail

What is special about this popular California tourist destination? Why has the US Government set aside this land so that people can visit here and explore? Research online and share what you learn:

1

2

3

4

ONLINE SOURCES OF INFORMATION:

_____

_____

National Parks

Search online for ten interesting facts about national parks.

1.

2.

3.

4.

5.

6.

7.

8.

9.

10.

ONLINE SOURCES OF INFORMATION:

_____

_____

Protecting the Land

Search online for ten ways that we can protect the land and its natural inhabitants.

1.

2.

3.

4.

5.

6.

7.

8.

9.

10.

ONLINE SOURCES OF INFORMATION:

_____

_____

Countries in North America

Use a phone, tablet or laptop to identify some of the largest and most populous countries in North America:

Belize, Canada, Costa Rica, Cuba, Dominican Republic, El Salvador, Greenland, Guatemala, Haiti, Honduras, Jamaica, Mexico, Nicaragua, Panama, United States of America,

Greece

Use a phone, tablet or laptop to learn interesting facts about this country.

Draw the flag for this country.

List five facts you discovered:

1.

2.

3.

4.

5.

List five common wild animals.

Describe a typical resident of this country

Draw a picture that best describes this nation.

Sources: _____

_____

California Forest Fires

How do forest fires start in the forest? How would early <u>pioneers</u> and <u>adventurers</u> escape the **flames** and **smoke** from a raging fire? Did humans accidentally start some of these fires? How?

ONLINE SOURCES OF INFORMATION:

The Wildlife of Illinois

Draw the state bird, tree, flower and insect of Illinois. Use colored pencils, crayons, or markers. Be neat and accurate.

Bird

Tree

Flower

Insect

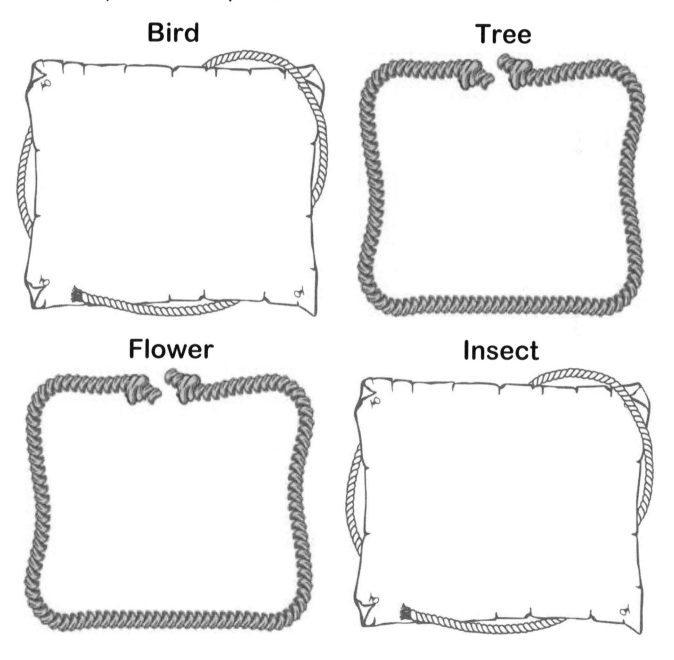

Interesting Facts about Japan

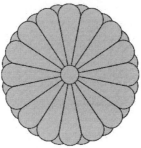

Use a phone, tablet or laptop to discover eight interesting facts.

1

2

3

4

5

6

7

8

Sources:

World Radio Day

World Radio Day

Use a <u>laptop</u>, <u>tablet</u> or <u>phone</u> to access the internet and explore **radios**. Record several interesting facts you learned about radios and this celebration on February 13th.

The Komodo Dragon

Use a phone, tablet or laptop to answer these questions.

Is the komodo dragon dangerous to humans?

☐ – YES

☐ – NO

_____
_____
_____
_____

How does a komodo dragon eat?

_____
_____
_____
_____

Is a komodo dragon smart?

YES NO

_____
_____
_____
_____

How long does a komodo dragon live?

_____
_____
_____
_____

24 365 7

source: _____

source: _____

source: _____

The Quechan Tribe

What is special about this indigenous tribe of California? Go online and search for information about their <u>history</u> and <u>people</u>, their <u>religion</u> and where they <u>lived</u>, their <u>leaders</u> and the <u>language</u> they spoke.

_____

_____

_____

_____

_____

_____

_____

_____

_____

_____

_____

_____

ONLINE SOURCES OF INFORMATION:

_____

_____

Illinois' Culture

Use a phone, tablet or laptop to discover interesting facts about this state.

Food

Music

Clothing

Sports

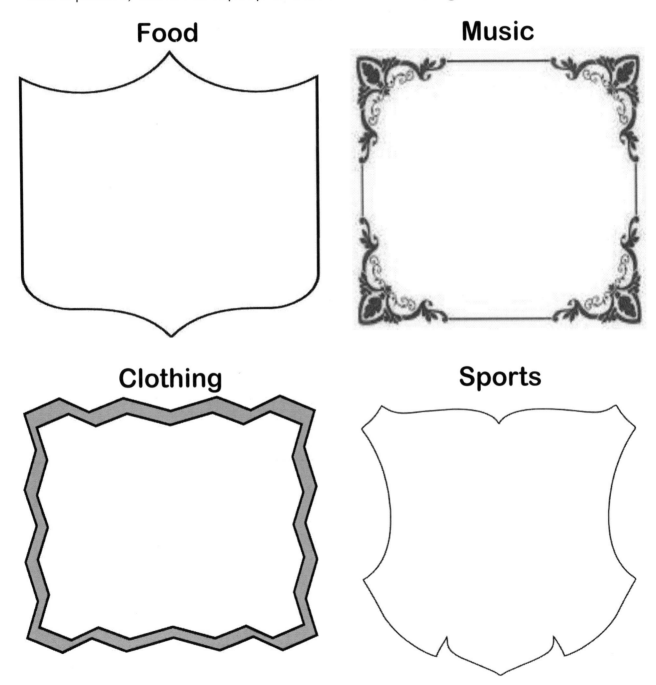

A U.S. Representative

List ten activities or actions that a US Representative is responsible for:

1.

2.

3.

4.

5.

6.

7.

8.

9.

10.

SOURCES:

_____

_____

The Salinan Tribe

What is special about this indigenous tribe of California? Go online and search for information about their <u>history</u> and <u>people</u>, their <u>religion</u> and where they <u>lived</u>, their <u>leaders</u> and the <u>language</u> they spoke.

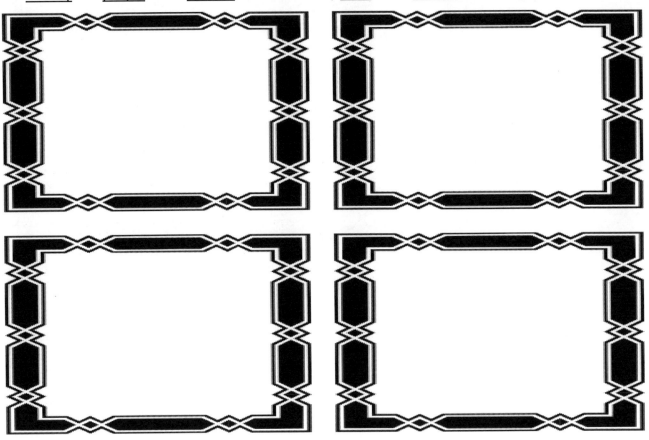

ONLINE SOURCES OF INFORMATION:

_____

_____

Interesting Facts about Texas

Use a phone, tablet or laptop to discover eight interesting facts.

1
_____
_____

2
_____
_____

3
_____
_____

4
_____
_____

5
_____
_____

6
_____
_____

7
_____
_____

8
_____
_____

Sources: _____

_____

Trinity College (Dublin)

Search for interesting facts about this Irish tourist destination. What are its most interesting features? Why do people travel there and explore? What is so amazing about this place?

 1

 2

 3

 4

ONLINE SOURCES OF INFORMATION:

_____

_____

The California Redwood

California State Tree

Use a <u>laptop</u>, <u>tablet</u> or <u>phone</u> to access the internet and explore this **tree**. Record several interesting facts you discovered in your research.

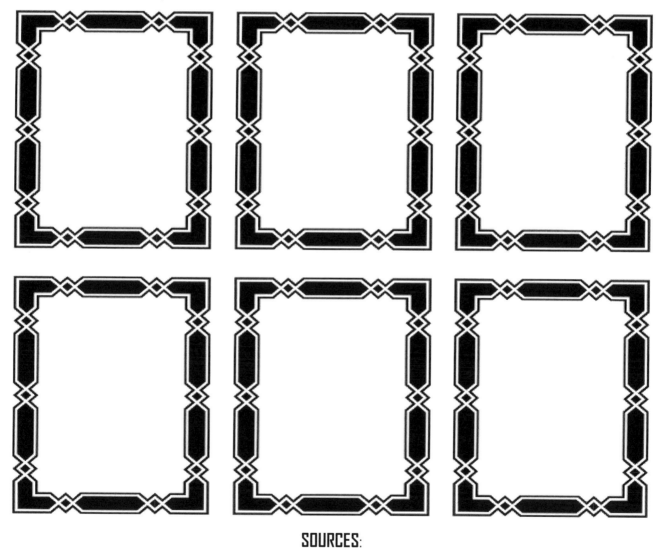

SOURCES:

_____

_____

The Serrano Tribe

What is special about this indigenous tribe of California? Go online and search for information about their <u>history</u> and <u>people</u>, their <u>religion</u> and where they <u>lived</u>, their <u>leaders</u> and the <u>language</u> they spoke.

ONLINE SOURCES OF INFORMATION:

Who is Antonie von Leeuwenhoek?

Use a phone, tablet or laptop to learn five facts about this scientist and why he is remembered today.

1 _____

2 _____

3 _____

4 _____

5 _____

SOURCES:

_____

_____

Countries in the Middle East

Use a phone, tablet or laptop to identify the countries of the Middle East:

Egypt, Iran, Turkey, Iraq, Saudi Arabia, Yemen, United Arab Emirates, Israel, Jordan, Palestine, Lebanon, Oman, Kuwait, Qatar, and Bahrain.

The Great Lakes of Illinois

The Shasta Tribe

What is special about this indigenous tribe of California? Go online and search for information about their <u>history</u> and <u>people</u>, their <u>religion</u> and where they <u>lived</u>, their <u>leaders</u> and the <u>language</u> they spoke.

1

2

3

4

ONLINE SOURCES OF INFORMATION:

Volcanoes in Hawaii

Internet Safety

1

Do your work. Don't play around. You have an assignment to do, so focus your attention where it is supposed to be.

2

Search for answers to the questions. Don't get caught going down rabbit holes in search of weird or strange stuff.

3

Imagine that your mother is sitting on your right and your teacher is sitting on your left, watching what you're doing. What would they say to you right now? Make good choices.

This workbook is part of a series:

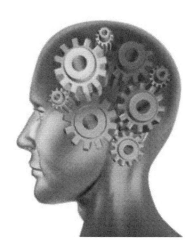

✓ Back to School Internet Research Projects (Grades 5-8)
✓ Christmas Vacation Internet Research Projects (Grades 5-8)
✓ Spring Break Internet Research Projects (Grades 5-8)
✓ End of School Internet Research Projects (Grades 5-8)
✓ Summer Vacation Internet Research Projects (Grades 5-8)
✓ Middle School Internet Research Projects (Grades 5-8)
✓ Junior High Internet Research Projects (Grades 5-8)

Each workbook is filled with 101 different activities to explore animals, people, foreign countries, U.S. states, athletes, singers, politicians, actors, holidays, Native Americans, postage stamps, coins, flags, maps, and so much more. All are available at Amazon.

Made in the USA
Middletown, DE
09 June 2020

97088141R00060